Contents

◇ Introduction

"Because of the research and curricular concerns that evolved from the previous decades, current leaders in the field of mathematics have encouraged the development of mathematics curricula that would more closely consolidate the understanding of mathematical patterns and structures simultaneously with computational competence and realistic application in problem-solving."

Gary Owen Bunch *The curriculum and the hearing-impaired student*
College Hill Press (1987)

The introduction of the National Numeracy Strategy (DfEE 1999) underlined the importance of mathematics in a broad and balanced curriculum for all pupils. Mathematics is no longer a subject in which drill, rote learning and memorisation are key strategies. Priorities of teaching mathematics include technology, problem solving, cooperative learning and the ability to apply mathematical understanding across the curriculum.

With the introduction of the National Strategy to Key Stage 3 (DfEE 2001), it is important that the skills and mathematical understanding of deaf pupils should continue to improve in line with that of their hearing peers. Most deaf pupils receive their education in mainstream schools although a number are educated within special schools for deaf pupils. Inclusion of all pupils into schools and into society in general is best realised when teaching and learning result in appropriate achievement by children.

These materials are designed to support the education of deaf pupils in both mainstream and special schools.

◆ The significance of Universal Neonatal (newborn) Hearing Screening (UNHS)

If the acquisition of many of the skills needed by deaf children is linked to a child's early experience, then the practice of screening all newborn babies for significant hearing loss is of immense importance in its potential for effective early intervention. This intervention must ensure, through parents who are well informed about deafness and its educational implications, that crucial information is available to deaf infants either through amplified residual hearing (hearing aids), a cochlear implant and/or early development of sign language.

The practice of continuous assessment and regular videoing of parent/child interactions by early intervention services for deaf children and their families offers vital opportunities for ensuring that those interactions cover all the mathematical information present in human experience and conversation. This will enable the deaf baby to begin to attend to all phenomena in the environment while parents learn to assume nothing but make information available by conversing through speech or sign with their child.

"...the field of deaf education, as a whole, must recognise the significance of mathematics knowledge and make mathematics education a priority."

Pagliaro C *Mathematics reform in the education of deaf and hard of hearing students*
American Annals of the Deaf, Vol 143: 1 (1998)

GUIDELINES LINK

*Effective early intervention
for deaf children 0-5
and their families*
RNID (2001)

◇ The importance of numeracy for all children

> *"Literacy and numeracy equip us with tools which allow us to surpass our natural limits of memory, perception and processing capacity amongst other things. They offer us new objects for thought, and these become frameworks for thinking that can be used for further learning."*
>
> **Nunes T** *Developing children's minds through literacy and numeracy. An inaugural lecture*
> **UCL (2000)**

All children need to acquire the concept of number and skills in counting while developing an understanding of quantity and how the application of processes such as adding, subtracting, multiplying and dividing may change it. There is both fun in the development of counting skills for young children and a more serious side whereby the child is acquiring a particular perspective on his/her experience, an early sense of logic and very practical tools for life.

Once the basic concept of number is secure, a child may go on to develop higher skills in mathematics and many children demonstrate a talent for understanding mathematical processes that can lead them on to the acquisition of highly developed problem-solving skills. For all children, however, the skills of mathematics are necessary tools for making sense of and contributing to their environment and conventions of society.

All children need skills that enable them to comprehend the importance of concepts such as:

- number
- quantity
- sequence
- groups
- size
- area
- capacity
- shape
- space
- mass
- length
- height
- growth
- time
- age
- money
- value
- possibility/probability
- relativity

Once such concepts are intuitively understood, children go on to acquire the analytical skills they need for problem-solving by discerning, calculating and manipulating the mathematical properties of all such building blocks in their world.

◇ Teaching mathematics to deaf children

"...life begins teaching fundamental mathematics skills long before children meet their teachers."

Stewart D A and Kluwin T N
Teaching Deaf and Hard of Hearing Students Content, Strategies and Curriculum
Allyn and Bacon MA (2001)

Teaching
mathematics
to deaf children

The teaching of mathematics is not an easy task, whether teaching deaf or hearing pupils. Yet no one would dispute the fact that ability in this ubiquitous subject is essential for all children. Young deaf children also need to see the world from different perspectives. The deaf child, like the hearing child, needs to develop flexible thinking skills early through explanation of as many different experiences as possible.

Almost all mathematical information is visible, occurring in space. We express mathematical information through language and other symbol systems, but the phenomena themselves are perceptible, eg angles (corners), and may be seen everywhere. Language, spoken or signed, is the vehicle for information and explanation. It is this essential information that assists the young deaf child to incorporate into his/her thinking those aspects of the tangible and perceptible world that s/he might otherwise be compelled to simply accept. Not giving information to a deaf child may teach that child to ignore a phenomenon, or particular characteristic of it.

For instance: 'Grandfather' appears quite different to a child from his/her parents. A child will accept visual differences and relate accordingly. However, grandfather is not just a different person – there are characteristics about him and his relationship to the family that can only be explained by his age. It is necessary, therefore, to explain age to a deaf child who can see the differences but needs the language in order to express what s/he sees and to link its relevance to the full picture of grandfather.

The hearing child will acquire this perspective on age through:

- asking questions about grandfather
- hearing conversations about grandfather and/or other children's grandfathers
- hearing conversations about different people and their respective ages
- learning that grandfather is daddy's or mummy's father
- celebrating grandfather's birthday
- hearing stories grandfather tells of his experiences when he was young
- hearing stories in which grandfather is a character, eg the children's classic Heidi.

If a deaf child does not have this same kind of information made available (to an even greater degree) then it may be some time before aspects of Grandfather are explained. In consequence, the child's appreciation of all that means 'grandfather' will have been limited. In the same way, the deaf child's perceptions of his/her world will have lacked a dimension and that fullness of explanation which hearing children receive without anyone doing anything out of the ordinary.

A deaf child's ability to acquire later mathematical skills will depend heavily on the child's early experiences and on a growing understanding that the abstract language of number, eg age, simply expresses one aspect of reality.

In addition, the practical tools that accrue through understanding the mathematical dimension assist us in solving problems. Developing this problem-solving approach to the world is an invaluable skill to both the deaf and hearing child alike.

It is this kind of mathematical foundation that all children need if they are to:

- develop the ability to form perspectives
- manipulate things they need to change
- think flexibly about situations that will be encountered while acquiring all kinds of knowledge, eg situations can be altered and we need to know not only how to make changes but if and when to make changes
- recognise illogical statements or reasoning.

The deaf child needs essential, linguistic information that incorporates this mathematical perspective.

As with all other situations in which information is being made accessible to deaf children there are crucial factors within the approach being used.

For auditory-oral children these include:

- hearing aids or cochlear implant and personal FM (radio) systems
- the acoustic environment in which aids are worn
- the language used by adults.

For children using signing approaches, crucial factors include:

- visual imagery and information
- the signing skills of parents, teachers or other adults.

The range and diversity of deaf pupils in mainstream schools are specified more fully in other guidelines materials.

Teaching mathematics to deaf children

GUIDELINES LINK

Effective inclusion of deaf children into mainstream settings
RNID (2000)

Using residual hearing effectively
RNID (2000)

◇ Early opportunities for introducing deaf children to mathematics

Early opportunities for introducing deaf children to mathematics

Teachers and parents of deaf children may be inclined to think that the main reason why some deaf children demonstrate very real difficulties with mathematical processes in school is because of the language of maths. It is clear to teachers of the deaf that deaf children do not necessarily have cognitive impairment. The real abilities of the children to deal flexibly with conceptual information may be hindered by the inaccessibility of other people's responses to phenomena, such as an exclamation of surprise or dismay, and to insufficient explanation of all that they perceive from their earliest awareness.

The written word can be adapted. A limited ability to think flexibly may be more linked to an inadvertent neglect of the mathematical dimension and perspective when providing the child with spoken or signed conversation in the early years.

Early concepts that are mathematical in nature or contain a mathematical perspective include:

- rhymes and patterns
- music and rhythm
- shapes – including angles
- colours – the number of colours in the rainbow, flowers, T-shirts
- shades of colours and terminology – light blue, dark blue, sky blue etc
- time and schedules, eg time for bed
- sequences – after this, then that
- turn taking – in games
- sharing – cutting an apple into so many pieces for siblings or friends
- having an extra piece or "One left over…"
- matching – the number of friends and the number of apple pieces
- matching type to type – 'That's the same as…'
- grouping – "Let's put all the apples in this bowl and all the oranges in that bowl"
- comparing – smaller than etc.

As with all other information in a child's early years, parents are the most natural and best providers. Once parents understand the importance of the mathematical perspective in their child's thought processes, there is a wealth of things around the home and in the child's world which they can use to stimulate their child's thoughts. Their role as main providers of vital linguistic information is crucial to their interaction with their child and to his/her development.

Mathematical information around the home includes:

- number – "Let's count the steps…one, two, three etc." "How many buttons on your shirt?" etc
- length – "We can't put those flowers in that vase – (demonstrate!) – they're too long."
- comparison – "Let's get a bigger vase."
- growth – most children will have a growth chart and this should be used on a regular basis just as with a hearing child – "You're taller than Aisha now."
- learning nursery rhymes, eg "Insy-winsy spider…" with actions
- teeth falling out (siblings) – "S/he's losing all her/his baby teeth one by one."
- money for ice-cream etc
- shapes, eg right angles on windows, the geometric posting box, road signs
- the car needing petrol – how do we know, how much do we need, where will we get it? "Let's go and pay the cashier!" (The child needs to be included in the whole business of getting petrol for the car etc)
- the sand pit – how many bags of sand are needed to fill it? (Parents may be tempted just to fill it and may need to learn to include their child in all activity such as filling the pit)
- the paddling pool – how long it took to fill it with the hose, or the number of buckets of water that were needed ("It's still not enough!" or "It's not deep enough yet." etc).

◆ Making the language and vocabulary of mathematics accessible

Many factors affect how very young children gain information and experience day-to-day conversations about mathematical ideas. For the very young deaf child, accessibility will be influenced by his/her degree of deafness.

However, information can be made more accessible to a deaf child when:

- a consistent level of amplification is maintained
  - by adults ensuring that the child's hearing aids, cochlear implant and/or personal FM (radio) systems are used well in each situation
- background noise is reduced
  - so that the listening environment allows children to make full use of their residual hearing
- children can see the faces of the people who are speaking
- adults avoid speaking in single words
  - by providing a clear stream of spoken language, delivered at natural pace, with modulations of stress and intonation
- adults are fluent users of British Sign Language (BSL) or the communication system being used
  - ie when conversing with children who use BSL, or sign communication to support spoken language

- adults repeat what they say in a natural, flexible way
  - by 'talking around the topic' rather than by constant repetition of the same sentence
- adults are alert to children trying to initiate conversation
  - or when they try to ask a question with limited expressive language
- adults provide good feedback to the child who tries to respond to a question whether or not they are right.

Teachers and parents should understand and take into account that deaf children characteristically:

Develop English vocabulary more slowly than their hearing peers and so require adults to pay more conscious attention to this aspect of development than they might otherwise do. Balancing the amount of repetition needed while consolidating vocabulary that is already familiar is a skill that must be developed. Parents need consistent encouragement to extend the range of words that are understood and used by their child.

Need visual clues and support to make what is being said to them meaningful. Adults conversing with very young children can learn to respond to this need by moving objects as they count them, pointing to children as they count them or by moving shapes and objects very clearly into clusters when children are looking for patterns and sorting into groups. Drawings, labels and written language all help and can be used from the early years onwards.

Need help to manage the issue of divided attention. Adults must be aware that children cannot look at the person speaking to them and at the objects or shapes being discussed simultaneously. They need time to look at objects, think about relationships and receive information from adults as they look at and attend to the speaker.

These are general points about how deafness impacts on language development and learning and they are covered in more detail in other titles within the Education Guidelines series.

◆ Learning to count at home

The parent or teacher who wants deaf children to build into their thinking the ideas explored above and many more mathematical concepts will quickly learn not to make assumptions about how the child will learn. The danger is that in the absence of information, the deaf child cannot learn appropriately and so is assumed to have learning difficulties. Deaf children – even where there may be other real difficulties – need to be fully included so that understanding, achievement and enjoyment of conversation and meaningful activity become an automatic and regular part of their child's experience just as they automatically become so for the hearing child.

The comparative wealth of information that the hearing child receives through constantly overhearing adult conversation, casual remarks and asides, radio

GUIDELINES LINK

Effective early intervention for deaf children 0-5 and their families
RNID (2001)

Promoting literacy in deaf pupils
RNID (2001)

Early opportunities for introducing deaf children to mathematics

and television programmes, is phenomenal. This information can only be provided for the deaf baby and young child if parents and teachers learn to use all naturally occurring situations and engineer other situations so as to provide that full explanation of how things come to be as they are. The cardinal rule is: "Don't leave the deaf child out."

The teacher of the deaf and parents working together will observe how:

Early opportunities for introducing deaf children to mathematics

- a deaf child's attention sometimes needs to be engaged through generating talk or sign conversation about an activity

- opportunities for meaningful communication present themselves when the deaf child is intrigued by something and turns his/her gaze towards the adult

- mathematical thinking skills are developed through play and practical experiences that are enjoyed by the child

- manipulative materials such as plasticine, clay or building blocks are the foundations of mathematical learning at this stage – enabling children to manipulate with their hands in order to learn practically those operations they will later need to perform in more abstract forms

- logic in reasoning may be developed through the mathematical perspective.

All children learn through play. A fun approach is the one best suited to the home situation and parents can use many activities and counting games in which the child will happily participate. The teacher of the deaf will ensure, by helping parents to be relaxed about these activities, that no anxiety arises, eg because the child gets the sequencing of numbers 'wrong'. That is all part of the process of building a mathematical understanding.

As the child continues to receive information s/he will be enabled to process that information.

Fun number activities at home may include counting:

- steps on staircases

- buttons on clothing

- types or colours of shorts, dresses etc

- how many people for mealtimes – places, forks, spoons, knives etc

- ingredients for cooking – weighing, measuring

- an amount of pet food

- with a tape measure or ruler and always being very particular about where the start of the measurement is, ie at the first line that equals 0, not at the tip of the ruler, and the end point of the measurement where it takes the full length of the ruler

- sweet or snack rations for each day of the week
- days until some event is due by using a calendar, incorporating pictures where possible
- minutes to bedtime or mealtime by using a clock
- while singing nursery rhymes that have sequences or numbers, such as "One, two, three-four-five! Once I caught…" "Hickory, dickory dock", "Five little ducks" etc
- while playing family games including snakes and ladders, ludo, draughts, dominoes, noughts and crosses and the use of dice etc
- counting while playing with an abacus.

It is also important to introduce the deaf child to the concept of zero by using phrases such as:

- it's all gone
- there's nothing left
- I don't have any
- there are none
- s/he has nothing
- s/he didn't get anything
- s/he scored zero
- we start at 0 (nothing or zero).

It is important that the child is introduced to as many family colloquialisms as possible so that the many ways of expressing the same idea are used naturally and interchangeably.

In all these activities the deaf child will acquire important skills while being actively engaged in learning rules or conventions and how they operate. Perhaps more importantly the child is acquiring the linguistic information that helps him/her to understand more fully the phenomena and activities experienced.

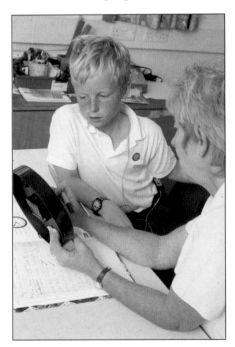

Expectation is a useful tool to involve the child in all family activities and in the importance of time and schedules. Children are active learners and enjoy the intuitive sequencing inherent in most family-centred occasions. It is essential for the deaf child to be an active participant.

In order to use expectation the parent may:

- make a rough order/schedule for the day ahead

- use a clock to link activities to time
- include some of the child's preferences in the schedule, eg watch *Teletubbies* at 10 o'clock
- ensure the child understands those activities that will involve 'going out', eg "Go shopping at 11.30"
- build sequencing into these expectations, eg "After we've done the shopping we will come home, have lunch and then you will have a story."

In this way the deaf child is not frustrated when, absorbed in a building block or puzzle activity, television programme or video, s/he is suddenly whisked off to get dressed for activities of which there had been no expectation or warning.

Early opportunities for introducing deaf children to mathematics

Sample of activities that may be used in the home with pre-school children

Ideas for families include:

- Counting the plates, knives, forks that are needed for lunch

- Counting while going up or down stairs

- Singing, saying and/or signing nursery rhymes or songs

- Sharing out sweets

- Dressing – different sizes, eg "That's too small for you now."

- Colours, eg "It doesn't really match but you like it, don't you!"

- Pouring drinks – "We mustn't fill it too full!"

- Play-dough while baking – cutting shapes – long, short, big, small etc

- Recognising door numbers

- Using magnetic numerals

- Using clock numerals

- Reading number stories

- Counting teddies or toys

Compiled from material contributed by LEA advisory services for deaf pupils, December 2001

What about the symbol for nought?

0 is an important number and it is easier for children to see the pattern of numbers if they see 0 in its proper place.

0	1	2	3	4	5	6	7	8	9
10	11	12	13	14	15	16	17	18	19
20	21	22	23	24	25	26	27	28	29
30									

0 is the beginning of a family of 0s:

0	10	20	30	40	50	60	70	80	90	100
	110	120	130	140	150	160	170	180	190	200

Compiled from material contributed by LEA advisory services for deaf pupils, December 2001

0 0 0 0 0 0 0

What about nought?

0 0 0 0 0 0 0 0 0 0 0

0 is everywhere!

- the date 2000
- telephone numbers
- door number

and a perfect score!

Compiled from material contributed by LEA advisory services for deaf pupils, December 2001

Children also need to know that 0, when it means zero, has a number of names!

Compiled from material contributed by LEA advisory services for deaf pupils, December 2001

◆ Other mathematical activities at home

Counting is one maths activity but there are many other situations in the home that can be turned to effective use in developing a mathematical perspective in the young child. Most parents, unless they are themselves mathematicians, will look to the teacher of the deaf for advice to help them to maximise their opportunities initially, but may go on to develop their own skills intuitively. Some parents may also have had experience with older children – the important factor for the deaf child always being to involve the child as fully as possible in the whole activity.

Teachers of the deaf may offer advice on how to develop:

- mathematics through play – the pretend shop, baking and measuring out the ingredients

- visual/practical mathematical experiences such as matching, sorting, cutting out shapes

- child-friendly mathematical terminology including idioms like "Wait a minute. I'll be back in a moment. Maybe – I don't know for sure", etc

- turn-taking in communication or activities

- routines and conventions – breakfast, lunch, please, thank you, bathtime etc

- sequencing skills – "After this one comes that one," or "What happens next?" etc

- familiarity with interchanging cardinal numbers (1, 2, 3 etc) with ordinal numbers (first, second, third etc) – "We'll fasten your top button first," and alternating with counting the buttons as they are fastened etc

- recognition of illogical requests and acquisition of the skill of saying "I can't do that," or "That's not possible for now," – eg it's not possible to have an apple if there are only oranges – "If you really want an apple we'll have to go out and buy some." The child needs to be exposed to reasoning if s/he is to begin to reason in this way too

- a sense of the ridiculous – for which comics or cartoons are good sources

- the skill of taking nothing for granted and ensuring that information and explanation through language and reasoning are always available to the deaf child.

Further important concepts to develop through language/conversation include:

- place and position – linking to prepositions, eg "Your big ball is on top of the garage" – above, over, below, under, inside, outside, around, next to, here etc

- quantifiers – all, any, some, none, each, a lot etc

- the concept of time being expanded – later, after, finished, past, tomorrow, yesterday, next week, in the morning etc

- using connectives – if this, then that, "That is because you were good" etc

- asking questions – "How many do you have?" "Where did I put that?" "When will we go?" "Which one did you take?" "Why do you want that one?"

Asking questions could be said to be the essence of mathematics and science, or simply of learning. When we ask a question it is because we do not know the answer and have recognised our need for information or that there is a problem to be solved. Children like to be a part of all investigative activity and this curiosity and willingness to be an active participant is invaluable and should be fully exploited with deaf children.

Deaf children need to:

- be motivated to ask questions – and understand that this is how they get the information they need or want
- be encouraged to ask questions
- know how to ask questions
- learn which questions to ask
- know when to ask appropriate questions
- recognise, and be able to give, positive and negative answers.

Therefore, every opportunity needs to be taken to:

- answer a deaf child's question however the child 'asks'. A young deaf child may depend on his/her body language and facial expression to assist in asking but these postures and expressions may not initially reflect hearing people's more conventional ones
- model the full language of the question before answering it (even though the child's own language level may be a single word or phrase)
- sometimes make a chain of questions – "You've lost your beaker? Where were you playing? Were you in the kitchen? Let's look there," etc.

A sample of seizing an opportunity to encourage questioning might be:

Problem: The child picks up the last remaining orange segment on the plate and looks questioningly at the parent. There is only one segment and there are three people at the table.

Parent's response: "Oh, dear, there's only one bit left! There's one bit…and look, there are three of us…" (counting and pointing to each person in turn) "…three people and only one bit. Would you like it? Yes? Okay. I don't want it and Mummy doesn't want it. Yes, you have it."

Opportunities for mathematical language as children grow and learn

As children play they develop:

New skills –
cutting out shapes and models
developing a sense of symmetry

Climbing –
how many steps?
how high?

Imagination –
knights and ladies 'a long time ago'

Ability to think and plan using
logic and reasoning

Ability to create –
shape, colour, size
and perspective

Compiled from material contributed by LEA advisory services for deaf pupils, December 2001

Number language through playthings that are:

found in nature
"Leaves fall from the trees because of frost and wind."
"Leaves float to the ground because of gravity."
(Connections)

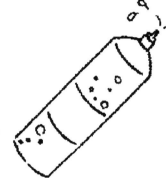

homemade –
for water play and fun

found in the home –
how long does the piece of string
need to be to tie up the parcel?

While communicating –
children learn to take turns, to give and take and to share

Compiled from material contributed by LEA advisory services for deaf pupils, December 2001

Suggestions that parents may use to teach essential mathematical language while playing with their deaf child.

Teaching mathematics through activities at home

- ## Counting

  Use everyday materials your child can see and manipulate when counting

  for instance, sweets, toys, steps, slices of bread for the sandwiches

  Sing songs such as: Five little ducks ... Five or ten in the bed ...
  Ten green bottles ... etc

- ## Comparing

  Play with objects of different shapes and sizes

  for instance, balls, teddy bears, building blocks, books etc and

  Use words about size – "That's the biggest ball. See if you can find a smaller one." or "Now you need three small blocks for the top."

  Use play-dough for making different sizes and shapes of imaginary objects "Let's roll the dough and make a long snake. Now make an even longer one. Which one is the shortest?"

  "This is a very big cake. Let's make some little cakes."

  Use stacking toys for finding out relative size and how things do or do not fit together. "It's too small for that part isn't it? Find where it fits."

- ## One-to-one matching/association

  When having a tea party, ask your child "How many people are there? How many cups and saucers will we need? Do we have enough cakes? Let's count them. How many more do we need? We need two more I think."

  While dressing Timmy teddy or Lucy the doll, "What do we need? Find some shorts for Timmy and a dress for Lucy. What else do we need?" etc.

Compiled from material contributed by LEA advisory services for deaf pupils, December 2001

◆ Mathematics at nursery school

The first day at nursery school is a milestone in the life of young children. The choice of nursery school for the young deaf child is a very important one and the teacher of the deaf will be able to offer parents information about what to look for when visiting potential nursery provision. Parents will be checking many aspects in relation to the needs of their child and should include, in their enquiries, questions about the approach used in stimulating and developing mathematics concepts and skills when making this important choice.

It will help parents, before they visit the potential nursery school, to know something about the early stages of teaching mathematical concepts that are most helpful to deaf children.

Parents should check whether the nursery school includes:

- an emphasis on hands-on experiences for children
- a focus on using visual and manipulative materials
- little or no reliance on workbooks or worksheets – even colourful ones
- stimulating activities for helping children to acquire the knowledge that is basic for the development of further maths skills
- an approach that encourages children to talk about how they did/made something, ie "Tell me/Show me how you did that."

Deaf children also require nurseries that cooperate to provide:

- good staffing ratios
- an appropriate acoustic environment
- in-class access support and/or sign language interpreters
- a cooperative approach in working alongside special needs support staff
- an inclusive culture that welcomes diversity.

The benefits of learning in the company of other children, where the learning environment takes their particular needs into account, can be considerable for young deaf children. Parents need to capitalise on all the experiences that a nursery school offers to their deaf child.

The teacher of the deaf may encourage parents to familiarise themselves with:

- the number of children in their child's class
- the names of all the children
- where all or some of the children live
- which children are particular friends of their own child.

All parents will want to know this information whether or not their child is deaf, but the objective behind this enquiry is particularly crucial for the parents of deaf children. Such information gives many opportunities for meaningful conversation where both parent and child are thinking of the same subjects though these are not actually present.

GUIDELINES LINK

Effective early intervention for deaf children 0-5 and their families
RNID (2001)

Early opportunities for introducing deaf children to mathematics

The teacher of the deaf may encourage parents to think of how:

- nursery school is the deaf child's main sphere of activity for lengthy periods
- nursery school teachers and playmates play a significant part in the deaf child's thoughts
- it is useful for the parent to point out where various friends of their child live, for instance, when on an outing in the family car. (Pictures of children will be helpful and can be kept in the car.)

Parents can then talk about:

- the comparative distance from where they live – close by, far off, a long way away etc
- distance from nursery school, eg "They're miles away!" "They're practically next door!"
- house numbers – the same number as M's, a bigger/smaller number than ours
- what time each child needs to leave home to reach nursery school.

The important factor for the teacher of the deaf is to strengthen and increase the parents' intuitiveness to incorporate the kinds of information that deaf children need to have, either through situations that occur naturally or situations that have been engineered. These strategies are essential if the deaf child's information bank is to be compensated for the wealth of repeated information hearing children get incidentally.

All such information regarding incidents or situations through which the deaf child is learning may be passed on to nursery school by means of the home/school book. Teaching staff can follow up this information through conversation and activities. The parent will be able to do the same when the home/school book comes home.

◆ Understanding number

> *"For most children practical work provides the most effective means by which understanding of mathematics can develop. It enables them to think out the mathematical ideas which are contained within the various activities they undertake at the same time as they are carrying out these activities; and so to progress ...from the handling of actual objects to a stage in which pictures and diagrams can be used to represent these objects...".*
>
> **Cockcroft Report** *Mathematics in the primary years. Mathematics Counts*
> **HMSO (1982) 1997, 10th impression**

Learning through practical hands-on experiences precedes all other approaches to mathematics learning. In the same way that children need to have full meaning when learning to read, so they need to understand what numerals are actually about. Simply attaching a word or sign to a visual symbol does not mean that a child understands what that symbol means in practical terms.

Although there may be books used in the home that introduce the child to the visual (picture) symbols of numerals alongside a matching number of objects, the names of numerals will only be meaningful to the child who has had many opportunities to experience counting. Children increase their learning through books but it is their involvement in practical activities that brings understanding.

It will be equally important that young children using British Sign Language (BSL) learn the signed numbers in this way so that, for instance, the sign for '2' also indicates two objects, not simply the numeral.

Concepts that are inherent in number include:

- quantity – how many?
- change (alteration) – take away, add to etc
- groups – apples, bananas, fruit (generic), cars, buses, trucks, vehicles (generic)
- elements – each unit within the quantity
- characteristics – colour, shape, weight etc.

Deaf children need to understand that within generic groups everything has a name of its own, eg:

- "You have four teddies now. They are called Rupert, Katy, Edward and Mop."
- "What a lot of fruit we have today – there are apples, pears, bananas and peaches. Let's count the apples first because there are lots of apples."
- "Let's put the crisps in the cupboard – salt and vinegar, cheese and onion" etc
- "Which cereal will you have for breakfast? Cornflakes, krispies?" etc.

The deaf child's need is not simply to experience all of these cognitive phenomena but to hear or see the language that expresses them, and all in a natural way that capitalises on real everyday experiences.

Whether at home or in nursery school it is useful for young deaf children to be involved in activities such as:

- finding as many 'blue' objects as possible
- counting all the spoons in the drawer
- looking for the missing spoon – "There are only five spoons here and there should be six. Where's the missing spoon?" (Great search) "Oops! Look, it's on the floor under the table."

Early opportunities for introducing deaf children to mathematics

- placing items in order of preference and using ordinal vocabulary, eg favourite colour/flavour of sweets – red first, then yellow second and orange third
- finding as many 'round' things as possible
- finding that round pegs don't fit into square holes etc –"It's the wrong shape!"
- deciding which of two or three objects is the 'heaviest'
- playing games that involve taking items away and finding how many are left
- separating fruit into types
- blowing and watching pillow feathers fly upwards then float down again – "That's gravity." (Hearing children don't understand either but we still tell them)
- flying a kite on windy days – "It's high in the sky!"
- blowing and bursting bubbles – "They don't last very long. Be quick..." etc.

All of the above activities and conversations should be accompanied by the appropriate family interactions undertaken in an atmosphere of fun and enjoyment so that deaf children are acquiring practical experience of number and the early vocabulary of mathematics simultaneously.

Early opportunities for introducing deaf children to mathematics

◆ Early mathematical language

"The way in which language is used in mathematical problems, where it often has very specific meaning, could also create problems. There is also a set of specialist vocabulary for mathematics."

Gregory S et al *Issues in Deaf Education*
David Fulton (1998)

In a child's early years the language of mathematics is descriptive rather than technical. It is a long way to travel from language such as "How many buttons are on your shirt?" to "The square on the hypotenuse of a right angled triangle is equal to the sum of the square on the other two sides." (Pythagoras) Teachers of the deaf may consider the age at which children become proficient in understanding the latter. By the age of 14 years, most pupils will have encountered Pythagoras' theorem, even if some of them find it difficult to understand or can see little relevance of that information (and some other mathematical concepts) to their lives.

One feature of the Pythagorean language is that it is very clearly mathematical. It is a code on its own, whereas the early language of mathematics is much more applicable to everyday life and experiences. How the language of mathematics graduates to become subject specific and how deaf pupils may be enabled to keep up with this metamorphosis is the challenge for teachers of the deaf and mainstream teachers who teach deaf pupils.

Examples of interchangeable terminology that deaf pupils need include:

- add, plus, in addition to, the sum of
- take away, minus, subtract
- problem, difficulty, dilemma
- answer, product, solution, probability (the latter may only be understood in relation to possibility and each concept's opposites such as unlikely/improbable and impossible).

This language of mathematics is not simply a matter of vocabulary, but of structures, and often those structures do not follow the intuitive norm.

For instance:

Question – "What is the difference between a number like 8 and a number like 9?"
Answer – "8 is an even number and 9 is an odd number."

Problem – "Find the difference between 10 and 13"
Solution – "3."

Teachers of the deaf need to plan with parents, nursery staff and Key Stages 1 and 2 mainstream teachers those strategies that need to be used to enable deaf children to learn progressively and to consider carefully the language of mathematics as they need and become ready for it. Teachers of the deaf also need to plan how to continue to expand language structures so that the child continues to build on practical foundations while learning to explore abstract mathematical terminology.

Strategies the teacher of the deaf may use include:

- planning in accordance with the child's interests
- teaching mathematical concepts in relation to known information
- focusing on what interests the child and highlighting mathematical properties in the conversation throughout an activity
- expanding the child's current knowledge through experiences
- teaching vocabulary and reinforcing with synonyms and multiple meanings (interchanging terminology naturally as often as possible and in as many situations as possible)
- assisting the deaf child by offering the wrong answer to cue the right answer (eg "What shape is a ring?" Where the child is having difficulty understanding the question, the teacher may ask "Is it square?")
- reinforcing success with additional examples.

Early opportunities for introducing deaf children to mathematics

If a deaf child's difficulty is with the format of a question and not with the concept itself, it is important that teaching strategies encourage the pupil to trust his or her own intuitive grasp of the situation and so, sometimes, deduce the question.

GUIDELINES LINK

Promoting literacy in deaf pupils
RNID (2001)

Promoting access to the curriculum for deaf pupils
RNID (2001)

Early opportunities for introducing deaf children to mathematics

It is essential to assist the deaf child to develop an understanding that:

- a question should be made clear to the listener
- it is sometimes necessary to have the question repeated or rephrased
- it is appropriate to persist until the question is clear
- answering the wrong question makes the answer wrong.

An underlying principle of the education of deaf children throughout the early years, and in accessing the curriculum, is the need to repeat the same things in every possible situation because deaf children do not 'overhear' other people's remarks or conversation. The deaf child's difficulty is not a cognitive one. It is about the need to access information in sufficient quantity and flexibly enough, ie through as many different situations as possible, to lay down a broad foundation of information about everything.

Teachers of the deaf, as well as mainstream teachers, need frequent opportunities to attend In Service Training and/or workshops on mathematics in order to upgrade continuously their own understanding of mathematical skills and teaching strategies.

◆ The beginnings of mathematical thinking

"Some of the words which are critical for developing mathematical understanding are the words with which deaf children have most difficulties, for instance logical connectives such as 'if' and 'because'."

Gregory S et al *Issues in Deaf Education*
David Fulton (1998)

From their earliest days hearing children learn about cause and effect because they hear. Deaf children will make such connections if the connection is clear to them either intuitively through another sense (ie vision, touch, smell or taste), or through explanation and/or demonstration.

Hearing children learn, through sound and language, that many things happen because of some preceding occurrence, and so logical connectives become a part of their intuitive knowledge of how the world operates.

Examples of occurrences that happen in response to a sound that may initially mystify a deaf child include:

- somebody picking up the telephone receiver because the telephone is ringing

- everybody running to the window because a loud bang has occurred outside
- a sibling going into the kitchen because the parent has called to him/her etc.

Examples of logical connectives a child makes may include:

- "If I don't behave myself, I won't be allowed to go to the party"
- "The vase fell off the table because it was not sitting properly in the first place"
- "The car crashed because it was going too fast around that corner."

Where this kind of linguistic information about occurrences and consequences is built into a child's thinking, such logical reasoning will form an important part of the basis that shapes the child's perspective on the world. Deaf children frequently understand more than they can express but the language (signed or spoken), given to explain and thus facilitate sequential thinking, enables the child to understand more fully. The deaf child is then equipped to express and/or demonstrate to others his/her intuitive understanding of situations and their implications.

Sometimes, simple observations the young deaf child offers may be implying the question, "Why?"

For instance:

- there are lots of blue flowers at the roadside, eg "Blue, blue, blue…" etc
- there are not so many red flowers, eg "Red…" accompanied by a pout or shrug
- the orange is round but the banana is curved, eg bringing the fruit to the adult and running a finger over each or saying the words, "Round" and "No!".

Such situations present opportunities to give a child responses such as:

- "I don't know why that is – but you are right."
- "I wonder why that is? Which colour do you like best?"
- "Let's look at all the fruit shapes when we go shopping." (Making sure to do so.)

As a deaf child acquires those experiences needed to view his/her world from a mathematical perspective s/he may begin to offer to others some logically connected information, eg:

- there is a spoon 'lost' because the quantity is wrong
- there is a button off a shirt and now there are only four buttons
- a sibling is at home when s/he should be at school
- a sibling is at home because s/he is sick
- broken glass is on the ground because someone dropped a bottle
- "I am good so I can go to the party."

Early opportunities for introducing deaf children to mathematics

Once a deaf child begins to point out to adults the patterns s/he perceives in the physical environment or in the family schedules and conventions, then intuitive mathematical thinking is occurring and needs to be developed by expanding these observations whilst celebrating the child's perspicacity.

◆ Mathematics through music and movement

Listening to tunes, singing and/or beating time to rhymes and rhythms and dancing to the beat are all as exciting and enjoyable experiences for deaf children as they are for hearing children. Visual apparatus such as flashing lights should be incorporated for children who rely on visual information.

Activities that encourage enjoyment of music and rhythm may include:

- playing games that depend on music, eg musical bumps, chairs, or statues
- keeping the tempo in rhymes and jingles – also may assist memory of words etc clapping to the rhythm
- marching in unison with the timing of the tune
- dancing and building in movements to coincide with the mood of the music
- playing instruments for fun such as bells, drums, chime bars etc
- forming 'trains' and making appropriate train noises rhythmically.

Deaf children need these experiences to begin to appreciate the facets of experience that help them to develop:

- their sense of rhythm
- a sense of timing and different tempos eg slow, fast, <1, 2, 3 > <1, 2 ,3 > or <1 and 2 and 1 and 2 > etc
- a rounded view of their place in society
- motivation
- a spirit of competition
- a sense of the fun and enjoyment in music and/or rhythm.

Early opportunities for introducing deaf children to mathematics

GUIDELINES LINK

Effective early intervention for deaf children 0-5 and their families
RNID (2001)

◇ What deaf pupils need in mainstream schools

> *"'Poor room acoustics are recognised as presenting a major challenge to any listener with a permanent degree of hearing loss' (Berg, 1993). Learning environments are frequently hostile to hearing aid users and as a consequence it may be assumed that special schools with acoustically treated rooms may have significant benefits. ...Such benefits can also be accrued within mainstream settings usually as a result of the intervention of ToDs and educational audiologists."*
>
> **Powers S and Gregory S et al** *A review of good practice in deaf education*
> **RNID (1999)**

Whatever the subject matter of lessons, deaf pupils will only benefit from being taught in mainstream lessons when they are able to access the information in the classroom.

Access to information for the deaf child is influenced by:

- the acoustic environment
- linguistic access
- visual access.

◆ An adapted learning environment

The acoustic environment

The acoustic environment incorporates both the pupil's own amplification system including FM (radio) equipment and acoustic treatment of classrooms in which lessons are taught.

A deaf pupil's equipment for access is the responsibility of the:

- parents who should ensure that the pupil comes to school with equipment in good order
- educational audiologist who must ensure the availability of spares and additional equipment for access to all educational information – where there is no audiologist, the teacher of the deaf takes this responsibility
- teacher of the deaf for daily checking and immediate replacement of faulty parts
- teaching assistant (TA) who will be assisting young pupils and observing when their auditory behaviour indicates run-down batteries etc

What deaf pupils need in mainstream schools

- class teacher who must utilise the additional equipment such as a pupil's personal FM (radio) system, or supervise the use of a conference microphone for groups
- class teacher or TA who should supervise the use of the FM system for the sign bilingual pupil while working in a group
- deaf pupil whose accountability will increase as s/he grows and develops.

Acoustic treatment of classrooms is the joint responsibility of the:

- school through the head teacher, SENCO and governors
- Head of Service for deaf pupils
- teacher of the deaf in a resourced school
- visiting teacher of the deaf in a non-resourced school.

Dependent on the number of pupils who use amplification and other technical devices served by a school, a mainstream school may consider the value of appointing an appropriately qualified technician able to service and check all acoustic/audiological and other equipment in the school – qualification in the audiological area being essential.

Linguistic access

Teachers who have deaf pupils in their class will be conscious of the pupil's need for spoken language to be clear at all times. This means that certain strategies are useful to bear in mind for use in all lessons that have been adapted for the inclusion of deaf pupils.

Such strategies include:

- always facing the class while talking
- using straightforward language
- standing in one place while speaking, to facilitate access to speech (lip) reading and facial expression
- repeating and/or clarifying contributions made by other pupils
- allowing time for the Communication Support Worker (CSW) to sign or fingerspell where necessary
- allowing time for the deaf pupil to respond
- changing activities to assist concentration.

GUIDELINES LINK

Using residual hearing effectively
RNID (2000)

Effective inclusion of deaf children into mainstream settings
RNID (2000)

What deaf pupils need in mainstream schools

Visual access

> *"It is not possible in this document to give detailed advice covering every type of special educational need. As a general guide, aim to include all pupils fully in mathematics lessons so that they benefit from oral and mental work and take part in watching and listening to other pupils demonstrating and explaining their methods and solutions. Identify relevant objectives from the teaching programmes, use suitable teaching strategies and give support so that pupils can access lessons."*
>
> **The National Strategy Key Stage 3**
> **DfEE (2001)**

Hearing pupils and deaf pupils in aural programmes receive most information through their sense of hearing even when there is a visual component in that access. Deaf pupils who cannot utilise hearing sufficiently or at all need equal access to relevant acoustic/auditory information, and must access that information by substitution of their sense of vision.

It is important that mainstream teachers understand the reason why visual information is as essential for many deaf pupils as auditory information is for others and that they know how to facilitate that access. The difference consists in utilising one sense for another so as to ensure that all relevant information is accessible.

What deaf pupils need in mainstream schools

Teachers of deaf pupils who use a sign bilingual approach in communication, including English for the written word, will need to:

- include the pupil by looking at him/her occasionally while teaching
- always look at the deaf pupil when addressing him/her
- understand that the pupil's eyes will be on the CSW
- understand that the CSW will voice-over the pupil's responses
- provide unrestricted view of the CSW for the pupil
- provide unrestricted access to all visual information in whatever form.

Visual access is essential for auditory/oral deaf pupils and incorporates classroom arrangements that allow the pupil to have an unrestricted view of the:

- teacher's face for speech (lip) reading and facial expression
- whiteboard, overhead transparencies, television etc
- faces of other pupils who are responding to questions, discussion etc (for groups, a horseshoe formation is helpful).

GUIDELINES LINK

Effective inclusion of deaf pupils into mainstream schools
RNID (2000)

Guidelines for mainstream teachers who have deaf pupils in their class
RNID (2000)

◆ Visual access for mental processes

"Pupils with hearing or visual impairments may need to be appropriately positioned in a class or helped to take part in an activity through signing or support by another adult. Other adaptations that may be necessary are, for example, preparation for oral and mental work…and the provision of materials that can be physically manipulated including the use of ICT and adapted measuring equipment."

The National Strategy Key Stage 3
DfEE (2001)

What deaf pupils need in mainstream schools

Visual presentation is the deaf pupil's means of access. Like their hearing peers, deaf pupils perform mathematical processes mentally but require the data to be presented visually.

Teachers of the deaf may assist mainstream teachers by:

- raising awareness of the need to present mental mathematics visually

- demonstrating how a set of flash cards is used, eg to test the 7 x table

- demonstrating how a set of flashcards may be designed to develop a deaf pupil's sequencing skills

- showing how to use a set of flashcards for the addition of three (or more) items

- showing how to use Information Communication Technology (ICT) to provide visual support when, for instance, the issue is about speeding up responses. (The question appears on-screen and when it disappears, the pupil must hold the question in his/her mind as the answer is worked out. The length of time for which the information appears on-screen is progressively shortened.)

It is important for the mainstream teacher to feel confident that:

- visual presentation for sign bilingual pupils, or any deaf pupil who relies heavily on visual information, gives exactly the same information as that received aurally by hearing pupils

- visual presentation is time limited

- it is only long enough for the pupil to assimilate, and that

- visual repetition is given as regularly as aural repetition

- hearing pupils understand the reason why visual presentation is necessary for the deaf pupil.

◆ Support for access – the teaching assistant (TA)

The TA, whose role is to ensure that a pupil is able to access the lesson content, will support deaf pupils in class.

The TA may use a variety of strategies to facilitate access including:

- ensuring that the young aural pupil's amplification equipment, or that of the young pupil using Sign Supported English (SSE), is in place and fully functional

- agreeing signals with the class teacher, eg to repeat where information has been missed

- ensuring that a task is understood where a pupil seems confused

- encouraging the pupil to respond in plenary sessions

- noting any areas of difficulty for the deaf pupil and discussing with the class teacher or feeding back to the teacher of the deaf who may need to address the difficulties in tutorial

- drawing diagrams or pictures to illustrate a process (having a small whiteboard available is one very useful resource)

- ensuring that homework is understood (the pupil should always ask the class teacher if anything is not clear) and that the home/school book, where appropriate, makes clear to parents what they need to know.

GUIDELINES LINK

Promoting access to the curriculum for deaf pupils
RNID (2001)

What deaf pupils need in mainstream schools

Strategies the teaching assistant (TA) may employ while supporting a deaf pupil in the daily mathematics lesson

The role of the teaching assistant (TA) can be to:

- observe the pupil's responses

- support the pupil in responding to the teacher

- support the pupil in responding in a group

- encourage participation by a pupil

- highlight key vocabulary

- offer help with specific resources

- encourage the pupil to ask the teacher for clarification

- help the pupil to maintain pace – but note if pace required is too fast

- clarify instructions

- note frequency of errors and discuss with class teacher

- clarify misunderstandings

- clarify numbers that may confuse, eg "Thirty – that's three zero"

- use flash cards to differentiate, eg 30 and 13

- facilitate independence wherever appropriate

- use an observation form for feedback to the teacher of the deaf.

The teaching assistant may need to be particularly sensitive to an individual deaf pupil's need or preference for a sense of 'distance' and ensure that support is arranged accordingly. The aim of in-class support for access is to facilitate a pupil's growing independence.

Compiled from material contributed by LEA advisory services for deaf pupils, December 2001

◆ Assessment and informed planning

"...assessment should be a continual and recursive process that makes use of multiple sources of evidence through the learning process."

Pagliaro C *Mathematics reform in the education of deaf and hard of hearing students*
American Annals of the Deaf Vol 143: 1 (1998)

Assessment of a deaf pupil's understanding of concepts and mathematical skills acquired will be essential when the pupil is entering school. The partnership with parents in this process will be invaluable. Assessments should be continual throughout school years, however, and less formal assessments such as module tests, quizzes and daily observations of a pupil may be highly informative in terms of interpreting formal test results and in planning the pupil's programme.

During Key Stage 1 the teacher of the deaf needs to make an assessment of a deaf pupil's abilities that may include how to:

- perform particular mathematical activities
- describe an activity
- use appropriate vocabulary
- carry out a task within a specified time
- count to 5, 10 etc
- count backwards
- perform mathematical processes such as add, take away etc.

The object of assessment in mathematics is to evaluate a pupil's mathematical skills and conceptual understanding. For deaf pupils, the level of language competence should not be allowed to get in the way.

It may be important therefore for informal assessments to be done while the pupil is actively and practically engaged in the tasks rather than conscious of 'being tested'. Arriving at 'correct' answers is less important than being able to describe or demonstrate the process used to obtain the answer. Wherever possible, the deaf pupil should be encouraged to describe the process. It is sometimes while explaining a process to another that understanding improves.

The point of assessment must be to ensure that a pupil understands:

- which process is required and why
- how to proceed
- how to analyse the process
- how to pinpoint where s/he went wrong and which part was illogical or did not keep to the necessary steps.

What deaf pupils need in mainstream schools

37

Reporting the results of assessment should stress:

- what the pupil can do
- areas of weakness
- those strategies teachers may adopt in assisting the pupil to reach another level of understanding and skill on the continuum of learning
- how parents may help at home.

The teacher of the deaf also needs to assess how a deaf pupil approaches the task set, for instance, whether the pupil:

- rushes at the task – often a sign of insecurity with the subject matter or the language
- works by trial and error
- is methodical
- looks carefully at the data provided
- attends only to key words
- cannot retain a number's integrity, ie keeps returning to count from one onwards when the sequence has been lost
- is precise etc.

What deaf pupils need in mainstream schools

The main purpose of ongoing assessment is to inform planning.

Mathematics and memory

Remembering a number

Children are often asked to remember a number and then count on or back. In the process, a child may forget where they started and some return to count from one onwards.

Memorising the number may be assisted by:
- verbalising the number
- tracing the number in the air (the child)
- marking the place on a number line with an object
- writing the number, for example on a 'post it', and sticking it on his/her hand or forehead to reinforce that this is the number that must be remembered.

Multiplication tables

While multiplication tables are usually learnt by verbal means, reciting them for instance, there are other ways that assist children to remember tables.

For instance:
- looking for patterns (a hundred square graph can help)
- colour coding – a different colour for each multiplication table
- overlays on 100 square to highlight a significant pattern
- encouraging younger children to walk/jump to the appropriate boxes of a large 100 square on the floor
- arranging a large class so as to form the pattern of a multiplication table
- using flashcards to show, for example 5 x 4 = ? and increasing speed by appropriately shortening the periods given for response.

Remember that activities that provide movement make use of the child's memory for movement as well as his/her visual memory. Recounting the activity involves story memory and this helps the child to memorise the sequence.

Number Bonds

The relationship between numbers is easier to understand if it can be shown visually. Cuisenaire rods, Stern, or homemade apparatus can also be used to help a child to see visually the relationship between numbers.

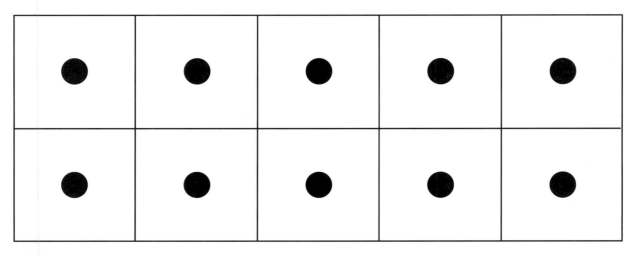

Cutting off one square can demonstrate the relationship between 1 and 9, that is 1 + 9 = 10 or 10 - 1 = 9, and 2 + 8, 3 + 7 etc.

Angles

ACUTE ANGLE
An acute angle is less than 90º

OBTUSE ANGLE
An obtuse angle is more than 90º but less than 180º

RIGHT ANGLE
A right angle is always 90º

REFLEX ANGLE
A reflex angle is more than 180º

STRAIGHT ANGLE
A straight angle is 180º

Compiled from material contributed by LEA advisory services for deaf pupils, December 2001

◆ Collaboration between teachers of the deaf and class teachers

The individual strengths and weaknesses of a deaf pupil in mathematics should form part of that pupil's Individual Education Plan (IEP). The appropriate amount of support and tutorial time specified should result from assessment and discussion between the teacher of the deaf, the class/mathematics teacher, the pupil and/or the pupil's parents, and be kept under review as the pupil progresses.

With this information the teacher of the deaf and the mainstream teacher need to:

- collaborate in planning the content and delivery of mathematics lessons which meet the needs of deaf pupils
- ensure that the Communication Support Worker (CSW) knows those mathematical signs that have been agreed for use in the lesson with the British Sign Language (BSL) pupil
- consider the pace of individual lessons
- consider the pace at which topics will be covered
- consider the practical explorations that might be used to introduce a new topic
- plan strategies for making best use of the teaching assistant (TA).

Where mathematics lessons are translated through the CSW into BSL it is imperative that signs to be used for mathematical concepts are agreed and used consistently throughout the school. The teacher of the deaf, CSW and class teachers need to collaborate to ensure this coordination.

It is important that mainstream teachers know how:

- the fingers used for signs to represent numerals in BSL are not random as with hearing children who use their fingers to count
- expecting young BSL pupils to learn to use the left hand for counting in conjunction with the signed number system on the right hand may be problematic[1]
- visual and/or manipulative materials will be more successful for the young BSL pupil in computation - a calculator may be used once the pupil demonstrates an understanding of the mathematical processes needed
- visual information may be central for the sign bilingual pupil when performing mathematical processes mentally.

In mental arithmetic, it is the process that needs to be performed 'in the head'. Giving information visually is a matter of access.

---

1   Reference: "The signed algorithm and its bugs" Nunes T and Moreno C in *Educational Studies in Mathematics 35* (1998)

Mainstream teachers' strategies that are particularly helpful to deaf pupils include:

- giving clear and direct instructions
- giving positive encouragement
- maintaining high demands
- maintaining 'busy' class behaviour with sensitive noise control where there are hearing-aided pupils
- regularly reviewing materials
- offering alternative activities
- accepting that visual information is essential for sign bilingual pupils even when the activity is mental.

The teacher of the deaf may incorporate tutorial sessions with a deaf pupil to consolidate concepts and ensure, through conversation and discussion, that the pupil is developing an understanding of mathematical concepts.

The teacher of the deaf may be managing a resourced base within a school and be regarded as a member of the school staff. The first priority will be to conduct assessments of each deaf pupil's understanding of mathematical vocabulary and concepts gained in the pre-school period, primary or middle school.

Where a deaf pupil is enrolled in a school that has no resource base, the pupil's needs will be the concern of the school's SENCO and class teacher/s through close collaboration with the visiting teacher of the deaf.

What deaf pupils need in mainstream schools

The signed number system 0-20

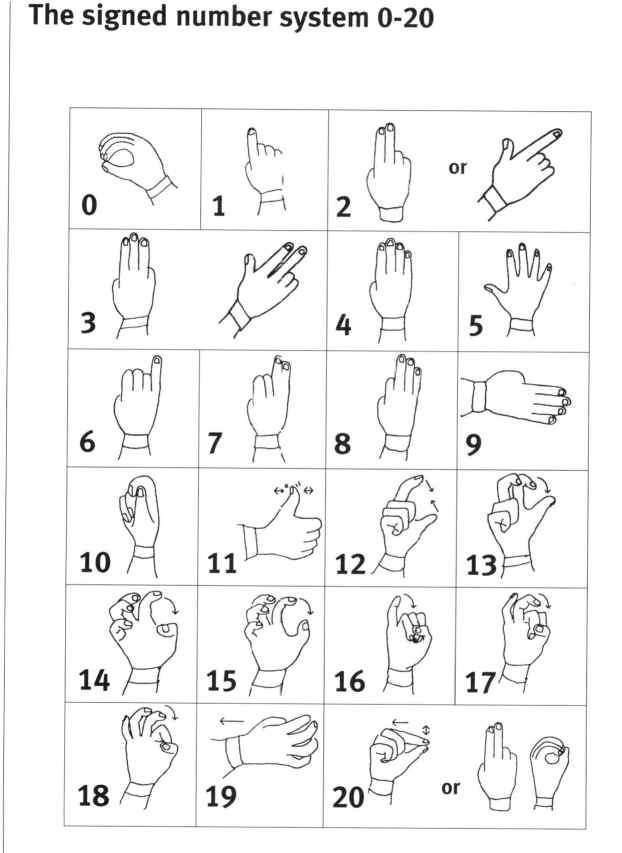

From: *Access to Maths*
Available from: The Jennie Lee Centre, Wolverhampton

Compiled from material contributed by LEA advisory services for deaf pupils, December 2001

The signed number system (tens) 20-100

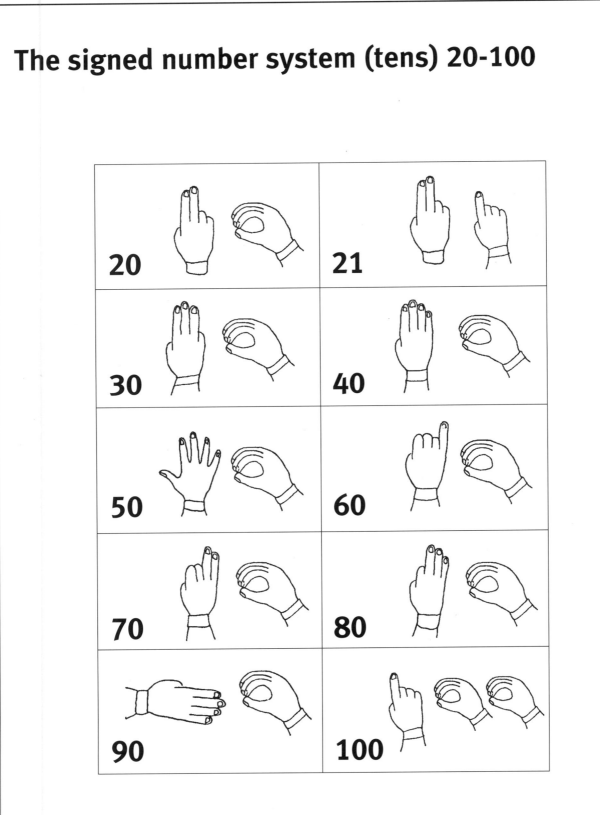

From: *Access to Maths*
Available from: The Jennie Lee Centre, Wolverhampton

Compiled from material contributed by LEA advisory services for deaf pupils, December 2001

The visiting teacher of the deaf in collaboration with the class teacher will be:

- using assessment information to evaluate a deaf pupil's knowledge and understanding of mathematical concepts
- assessing the appropriateness of a group for the deaf pupil
- ensuring that lessons are adapted appropriately for access by the deaf pupil
- planning appropriate support through the TA.

What deaf pupils need in mainstream schools

◇ # Using calculators and Information Communication Technology (ICT) in teaching mathematics

"...technology should be available and used as a tool to expand instruction and enhance understanding and knowledge. ...The Internet and innovative software should be included as tools that augment the learning environment and allow students better access to information in both written and visual form."

Pagliaro C M
Mathematics reform in the education of deaf and hard of hearing students
American Annals of the Deaf 143, No1 (1998)

◆ Calculators

Deaf pupils need knowledge of and access to a range of micro-technology including electronic calculators. The benefits of electronic technology to deaf pupils need to be weighed against possible disadvantages but, generally, visual access to information and the ability to work at an appropriate pace are particularly important to the deaf pupil who is continuously acquiring general and mathematics specific linguistic competence.

The teacher of the deaf in mainstream schools will be aware that:

- different views may exist about the appropriate use of calculators in teaching mathematics
- the school or mathematics department of the school may have their own strategies for implementing the use of calculators
- many pupils will have access to calculators at home or in their personal computers at home or in school
- electronic calculators play a significant part in modern industrial technology and therefore deaf pupils need to be adept in their use.

Benefits for deaf pupils through the appropriate use of calculators include:

- checking own calculations
- making frequent checks throughout a process
- being able to locate where s/he has gone wrong
- knowing when to seek help, eg because agreement is not occurring
- getting the right answer to a problem when the method was followed correctly.

It is important that the deaf pupil has a good understanding of quantity when using calculators for large calculations, so that the pupil can anticipate the approximate answer and quickly recognise an inappropriate amount.

Teachers of the deaf may need to stress to deaf pupils that:

- it is dangerous to assume that the answer on a calculator is automatically correct

- the data entered needs to be correct and checked on the display as it is entered

- employing different processes is a means of checking, eg by using subtraction, addition, multiplication etc

- reversing the order is another way of checking, eg 600 + 750 + 396 = 1,746

- may be re-entered as 396 + 750 + 600 = 1,746 – ensuring that answers correspond

- not all processes apply and they need to choose appropriate processes, eg 500 – 324 = 176 can be alternatively checked by addition but not by multiplication (a pupil's ability to choose appropriate strategies for checking is, in itself, evidence of the pupil's mathematical understanding)

- calculators can perform many mathematical operations provided the operator understands the necessary processes

- all calculators are not the same

- it is important and can be fun to find out what particular calculators can do.

◆ Information Communication Technology (ICT)

The visual and methodical nature of computer-assisted learning has distinct advantages for deaf pupils. The mainstream teacher, teacher of the deaf and teaching assistant need to be vigilant, however, to ensure that the deaf pupil is making appropriate progress. The deaf pupil should be acquiring and/or reinforcing mathematical processes and skills through the use of ICT.

Computers may be used effectively with deaf pupils in the teaching and learning of mathematics where software:

- meets specific learning objectives for pupils

- provides good visual demonstration of mathematical concepts

- enables deaf pupils to work independently and at their own pace, without falling significantly behind

- incorporates good question and answer techniques

- enables deaf pupils to interpret or explain results, ie encourages reasoning

- enables deaf pupils to handle data efficiently.

Benefits of ICT for a deaf pupil may include:

- having visual formulae for computation
- feeling under less pressure
- working at own pace
- having visual access to different types of graphs and their applications
- following a method
- self-correcting – no disapproval experienced
- finding visual presentation of linguistic content less ambiguous
- keeping a database (may also be used to assist in problem-solving).

As the program advances the teacher or TA may need to ensure that the deaf pupil asks for help whenever the terminology is unfamiliar so that the pupil's mathematical progress is not hampered by linguistic difficulties and their grasp of mathematical language for the appropriate level is also improving steadily.

The benefits of software need to be evaluated for each deaf pupil and this evaluation ought to show that a pupil is making greater strides in their learning and application of mathematical skills through the use of ICT than they would otherwise have done.

Software that is currently available addresses:

- counting skills
- sequencing
- all levels of computation
- logic
- algebra
- geometry
- probability etc.

The following software has been found to be particularly appropriate for use by deaf pupils:

NUMBERS

This program has no graphics but is excellent for reinforcing basic number skills.
From: Caves Ltd, PO Box 204, St Albans, Herts AL4 8JU

Dlk Place Value

A good program to help with the understanding of place value by dragging numbers on to a stone stair in ascending order. Numbers include
Positive numbers, +/- numbers, decimal numbers. £8.50 per module (52 mods)
E-mail: sales@dlk.co.uk

MicroSMILE for WINDOWS

Pack 2: Angle estimation – very useful and lots of fun.

Pack 3: Sense of number (10 different programs here) including place value of whole numbers, decimals, fractions and negative numbers.

Pack 8: Numeracy (nine programs). Straightforward practice and strategy games to apply numeracy skills and develop own strategies.

From: SMILE mathematics, The SMILE Centre,
108 Lancaster Road, London W11 1QS
E-mail: smile@rmplg.co.uk

MATHS Explorer CD

Aimed for KS2 but useful with KS3

Material on number, shape, space and measures, handling data, using and applying maths, probability and statistics, calculators and computers.
Granada Learning Ltd, The Television Centre, Leeds LS3 1JS

www.webcomde@fax.com
www.becta@becta.org.uk

Teachers of the deaf may use the benefits of ICT to exchange information with each other so that good ideas are shared widely and quickly by the profession as a whole.
E-mail: majordomo@ngfl.gov.uk

Using calculators and Information Communication Technology (ICT) in teaching mathematics

◇ The National Numeracy Strategy (NNS) – Key Stages 1 and 2

The National Numeracy Strategy (NNS) introduced to primary schools in 1999 underlines the importance of establishing a firm foundation in both mathematical thought processes and computational skills for all pupils if they are to go on to acquire higher skills in problem-solving.

◆ The daily mathematics lesson

A dedicated mathematics lesson has become part of the routine in primary schools.

The teacher of the deaf may need to assess the appropriateness of a deaf pupil's mathematical skill for involvement in:

- oral work and mental calculation (whole class)
- the introduction of new topics and/or consolidation (may be individual or in groups)
- the plenary session to consolidate the pupil's grasp of lesson content.

The emphasis that is placed on the understanding of mathematical concepts through reasoning skills, encouraging pupils to explain both their answers and how they arrived at these can offer valuable experience for deaf pupils in terms of language and mathematics. However, not all deaf children start school well equipped to respond linguistically and some deaf children may not have had experience of essential practical mathematics as outlined earlier in these guidelines materials.

For instance, some young deaf pupils may need to develop or extend their abilities to:

- sequence events
- understand and use positional vocabulary such as 'at the bottom of…', 'in front of…' etc
- understand and use ordinal vocabulary
- understand and see connectives
- know how to interpret the information given
- look carefully at all data.

Teachers of the deaf may need to ensure that some deaf pupils are developing necessary skills such as:

- attending to all data
- analysing and sorting necessary information from redundant information
- being able to explain why particular information is redundant
- focusing on relevant information
- a systematic approach
- being precise.

The teacher of the deaf may sometimes, in tutorial, conduct fun situations in which deaf pupils are presented with information that cannot be used to solve a particular problem. The aim of the session is to enable deaf pupils to recognise when information given is either irrelevant or insufficient.

For instance:

- A shepherd is 42 years of age. How many sheep does the shepherd own?
- Mrs X bought three kilos of sugar. How much did she pay for the sugar?

More subtle situations may gradually be introduced in order to assist the pupils to focus on the problem posed and the particular information that is required if a solution is to be found.

◆ Adapting the lesson – access for deaf pupils

As with all teaching for deaf pupils, classroom acoustics, the pupil's access to visual information and the pace at which the teacher's instructions are given are vitally important. The teacher of the deaf may assess a pupil's understanding of concepts that are being introduced or consolidated in class lessons.

For some pupils, it may be necessary to:

- give more time to mathematics teaching, eg in tutorial
- allow more 'on task' time
- provide visual/manipulative materials
- assess whether the pupil is ready for the level of abstract reasoning required
- assess the appropriateness of individualised activities.

Where a deaf pupil is having difficulty, it may be necessary to reinforce the pupil's understanding by:

- using other materials to broaden the pupil's experience
- continuing to teach to the pupil's strengths
- continuing to relate the concept to known information
- using the vocabulary and interchanging where possible with non-maths contexts.

GUIDELINES LINK

*Promoting access to the
curriculum for deaf pupils*
RNID (2001)

The teacher of the deaf may incorporate one-to-one tutorials for particular deaf pupils to:

- assess the pupil's understanding of fundamental mathematical concepts
- assess the pupil's understanding of those concepts needed for the particular level
- assess and, if necessary, assist the pupil's ability to express mathematical concepts
- assess the pupil's understanding of place value
- use strategies to consolidate understanding of place value where needed, eg an abacus and structural apparatus (worksheets are abstract and depend upon the pupil's practical experience being sufficient for transition)
- consolidate ideas so that pupils can express how they may solve particular mathematics problems
- assist a pupil who is having difficulty to envisage practical situations that incorporate the mathematical task involved, or engineer practical experiences for this purpose
- play informal maths games.

The National Numeracy Strategy (NNS) – Key Stages 1 and 2

Assisting access for deaf pupils in oral work and mental calculation

Benefits:

- provides opportunities to concentrate on oral, practical and interactive work that is not worksheet-based but involves a two-way process of discussion with adults or peers

- increases the emphasis on higher reasoning skills and open questions

- develops skills such as hypothesis, interpreting information, comparing etc.

Points to consider:

- a deaf pupil may process information more slowly than his/her peers and not be able to keep up with the pace of the lesson

- a deaf pupil may be accustomed to a more passive role and to closed questions.

Teaching strategies:

- ask questions that require an explanation rather than a yes/no answer

- build in a 'wait' time so that all children have the opportunity to think before answering a question

- match the complexity of the question to the skills of the deaf pupil

- use stories, rhymes and songs where appropriate to help with remembering facts or concepts

- use support staff to work with a small group with parallel questions but at a slower pace.

Compiled from material contributed by LEA advisory services for deaf pupils, December 2001

Assisting access for deaf pupils in the main activity

Benefits:

- structured activities allow work to match the individual need

- pupils can work towards their own objectives

- there are opportunities to make links between mathematics and other subjects.

Points to consider:

- the deaf pupil may have learned new mathematical terms, but s/he can still be confused by instructions that are too detailed

- deaf pupils may have difficulty transferring their knowledge and making links between subjects.

Teaching strategies:

- provide written materials, group tasks and homework that include:

  - worksheets that have pictures or diagrams

  - guided steps

  - simplified carrier language

- encourage pupils to work independently but clarify if there is a problem

- ensure equal partnership with a hearing peer that will benefit a deaf pupil in paired work

- use the pupil's Individual Education Plan (IEP) to guide group work with support staff.

Compiled from material contributed by LEA advisory services for deaf pupils, December 2001

Sample information for mainstream teachers with deaf pupils in their class

Assisting access for deaf pupils in the plenary session

Benefits:

- consolidation of learning points encourage the pupil to reflect on his/her achievements

- provides opportunities to listen to others and/or present findings

- homework that is based on learning can be set.

Points to consider:

- the pupil may have difficulty accessing the language or discussion

- the deaf pupil may not be confident or able enough to present or explain his/her own work

- homework requirements need to be heard, understood and written down.

Teaching strategies:

- ensure that the deaf pupil can hear and see as clearly as possible

- provide praise and encouragement

- allow extra time for support staff to practise presentations with the pupil if necessary

- use the home/school book to involve parents where needed for homework assignment, eg measure five items at home.

Compiled from material contributed by LEA advisory services for deaf pupils, December 2001

◇ **Mathematics at Key Stage 3**

> *"The challenge now is to secure and build on the pupils' achievements in Key Stages 1 and 2. The National Strategy for Key Stage 3 aims to address this challenge…".*
>
> **National Strategy Key Stage 3**
> **DfEE (2001)**

The introduction of the National Strategy to Key Stage 3 brings new opportunities for teachers of the deaf to be proactive in the implementation of this extension of the numeracy strategy. Through appropriate planning with the head of the mathematics department the teacher of the deaf who works in mainstream education may be involved at the earliest planning stages.

The teacher of the deaf needs to know:

- how interactive the mathematics lessons will be – desk work may not be the most appropriate for some deaf pupils and may require the teaching assistant (TA) to be present
- the topics to be covered and the approximate time-scale
- the assessment techniques to be used in the mathematics programme
- acoustic and visual adaptations that may be needed in classrooms.

Teachers of the deaf should ensure that pupils understand how mathematics is integral to experience and its themes are:

- not new at any given stage
- developed at different stages
- continuous as awareness increases
- recognised in new examples.

At the secondary phase, for instance, deaf pupils, according to ability, need to be increasing their understanding of:

- measurement and formulae – perimeter, radius etc
- estimation and approximation

- use of calculators
- graphs – constructing, interpreting, predicting from and understanding the relationships between different types
- data collection and reporting
- risk calculation based on probability
- the application of the particular to the general
- the importance of logical reasoning and the need for proof
- methods and formulae for problem-solving
- the significance of shapes and scale in geometry.

"Support staff, where they are available, can help to make sure that particular pupils participate in their mathematics lessons as independently as possible. The aim is still inclusion – support is not a substitute for careful thinking about including everyone in the lesson. The success of the support will depend on good communication and working relationships between the mathematics department and the staff managing individual pupil support."

National Strategy Key Stage 3
DfEE (2001)

Strategies that may assist the mathematics department to meet the needs of deaf pupils, in collaboration with the teacher of the deaf, may include:

- assessment that distinguishes linguistic difficulties from mathematical conceptual difficulties throughout the revision programme in year 7
- choosing an appropriate mathematics group for each deaf pupil that avoids either underestimating or overestimating a deaf pupil's understanding and skills
- planning to use a non-teaching period, perhaps once or twice per term, for the mathematics teacher to conduct a session for deaf pupils in the resource base – addressing particular difficulties where these are apparent
- discussing the role and skills of the teaching assistant (TA) so that deployment is appropriate and effective.

Mathematics at Key Stage 3

◇ The language of mathematics

"Mathematics did not invent the arcane, so the claim that the vocabulary of mathematics is a special problem for deaf children distracts from the real issue. Every child, deaf and hearing, has to learn the vocabulary. The issue with deaf children is how they are going to learn it."

Stewart D A & Kluwin T N *Teaching Deaf and Hard of Hearing Students-Content, Strategies and Curriculum*
Allyn and Bacon (2001)

Mathematics describes actual phenomena and processes. Both the description of and the application of mathematical processes requires specific terminology which lies outside the everyday language of most people. Teachers of the deaf and mainstream teachers need to consider how best to deliver this information in ways that deaf children can access too. Thorough familiarity with the vocabulary and linguistic structures of the mathematics' syllabus to be used in lessons is necessary in order that the teacher of the deaf can plan pre-lesson and/or post-lesson tutorial sessions to introduce or reinforce the language and terminology needed. All key terminology is to be found in the National Numeracy Strategy (NNS) (DfEE 1999) and NS Key Stage 3 (DfEE 2001).

◆ Vocabulary

The class teacher may provide a list of key vocabulary to the TA who should have strategies planned in advance for cueing the young deaf pupil when an otherwise familiar word is being used in a mathematical context, eg table, light. Many teachers display pictures around the room that include key words and the TA should ensure that the deaf pupil makes appropriate use of these.

A considerable amount of mathematical vocabulary has both general meaning and specific meaning, eg difference, product, solution etc. It may be helpful if teachers of the deaf assist deaf pupils to construct their own dictionaries in which they differentiate such vocabulary. Dictionaries of mathematical terminology may also be constructed in mainstream classes. However, the deaf pupils' dictionaries may need to differentiate in a way in which those of hearing pupils do not because of their intuitive understanding of language through unhindered exposure to spoken language from birth onwards.

When teaching unfamiliar or contextualised vocabulary, the teacher of the deaf will be:

- using what the pupil already knows
- using what interests the pupil
- providing synonyms or phrases that amplify meaning such as comparison, eg lighter than = not as heavy as, equal to = the same as etc

The language
of mathematics

- providing conversation that enables new concept words to be used meaningfully

- incorporating new words into a related activity such as an art or design technology (DT) or craft project, eg some angles tessellate but circles never tessellate

- ensuring that there are agreed signs for mathematical terminology that will be used consistently in class as in tutorial (some may be fingerspelt)

- including all new words appropriately in the pupil's dictionary – using clear explanation or definition and sign graphics as a bridge to English for pupils who use British Sign Language (BSL)

- ensuring that as the subject increases in complexity, deaf pupils will be introduced to appropriate vocabulary such as incidence, tangential, inverse etc and given sufficient opportunity to consolidate the meanings through conversation and discussion, eg "The car crashed by skidding off the road at a tangent that brought it up against the bollard." A sketch or diagram of the incident may be used to illustrate the tangent.

The language of mathematics

Sample of sign graphics

Pound

Money

Balance/Weight

Altogether

Pair

Half

Compare

Cheap

Day

Thick

Thin

Week

◆ Structure

The structures of language generally present deaf pupils with the greatest challenge, and their linguistic difficulties are increased by the use of specific terminology and conventions used to express mathematical data, problems etc. It is important that all teachers understand that linguistic difficulty in deaf pupils does not necessarily mean conceptual difficulty. Pupils often understand the task or process and its implications but cannot yet express these fully. It may also be the case that inadequately developed linguistic competence limits efficient memory and leads the pupil to miss out necessary steps in the process.

It may be helpful if the teacher of the deaf:

- encourages pupils to describe what they are doing as they are doing it
- encourages pupils to think out loud when in the resource base if it does not disturb anyone else
- models the language, spoken or signed, while working through the process with the pupil.

Teachers of the deaf may need to consider whether:

- enough time is spent on mathematics
- enough time is spent on particular topics within the mathematics syllabus
- language competence is sufficient for the stage reached in maths
- the Communication Support Worker's (CSW's) interpretation skills are equal to the information being delivered
- further adaptation is needed for access to the level of information offered
- the deaf pupil is given opportunity to express what s/he knows
- sufficient time is spent explaining where a deaf pupil has misunderstood or has made a genuine error, eg has omitted a crucial element and needs to recognise that that is why the process did not work.

Linguistic improvement may also be developed by encouraging deaf pupils to describe informally:

- how they are enjoying mathematics
- what tasks they find difficult
- why they like or dislike the subject
- what strategies would help them more in class
- whether or not mathematics helps them in other subjects, eg science
- how it helps them in other subjects, eg history or geography
- what jobs they might consider if they do well in mathematics.

GUIDELINES LINK

Promoting literacy in deaf pupils
RNID (2001)

The language of mathematics

◆ Logical reasoning and mathematics

"Basic skills in computation no longer suffice in the workplace, as the job market demands proficiency in problem-solving, cooperative work, and computer technology. For deaf and hard of hearing students in particular, a strong mathematics education may be a determining factor in their future, providing professional choice and increasing opportunities for advancement."

Pagliaro C *Mathematics reform in the education of deaf and hard of hearing students*
American Annals of the Deaf, Vol. 143: 1 (1998)

Research[2] on the mathematical skills of deaf children confirms that there are no cognitive reasons found to explain why deaf children should lag behind hearing children in mathematics.

Deaf pupils, like their hearing counterparts, need a well balanced mathematics programme that:

- goes beyond computational skills
- builds higher order processes on established mathematical foundations
- enables them to have confidence in their own intuitive assessment of situations/problems
- assists the transition from intuitive understanding of situations/problems to the application of analytical processes in resolving/solving them
- imparts confidence for working in groups or partnership.

The teacher of the deaf may ascertain each deaf pupil's ability to recognise:

- the names of all mathematical tools, eg protractor, compasses, the function of each tool and why that is the appropriate tool for a particular task – "Tell me what you need that for." "Why can't you use this instead?" etc
- the four basic mathematical operations and which operations are needed for solving particular problems – "Can you solve that problem any other way?"
- methods for solving particular problems and why those methods apply.

To develop a deaf pupil's mathematical perspective, the teacher of the deaf needs strategies that enhance a deaf pupil's ability to analyse situations/problems.

Deaf pupils need skills that enable them to:

- discuss problems/situations with others in groups
- recognise irrelevant/surplus information
- process relevant information

The language
of mathematics

2   Paul Arnold: Mathematics and Deafness in *Deafness and Development 1* (2) (1990/1) Nunes I and Moreno C: *Is hearing impairment a cause of difficulty in learning mathematics?* EQUALS 3 (1) 1997

- recognise where there is insufficient information to give a particular answer
- ask questions for clarification or to challenge an assumption
- reason logically
- see and make logical connections to related phenomena
- support reasoning with facts
- make decisions individually and cooperatively
- be able to offer proof.

One vitally important factor about the teaching of deaf children is in the consistency of building upon the pupil's experience. Additional experiences should be supplied where needed, to ensure that each deaf pupil has sufficient information to begin to make necessary connections and to see implications as hearing children do, and at the same age.

◆ Problem-solving and critical thinking

It is important for all children to succeed and deaf pupils need to experience success in the same way as hearing pupils. It is crucial, therefore, that the deaf pupil knows the processes for solving problems at one level of difficulty before being presented with more complex problems.

With sufficient knowledge and competent mathematical skills, the deaf pupil's main need is for increased linguistic access if his/her analytical and problem-solving skills are to be developed fully.

The mathematics teacher, in collaboration with the teacher of the deaf, needs to know each deaf pupil's aptitude for:

- recognising contextualised vocabulary
- taking note of all data
- being systematic
- reflecting before choosing the approach needed
- sorting relevant from irrelevant information
- controlling impulsiveness (it is important to consider why a particular deaf pupil is impulsive and to target the cause rather than the symptom)
- being precise and using a calculator to make periodic checks
- working cooperatively in groups or with a partner
- recognising and using the mathematical terminology required, eg hypotenuse, isosceles, tangent, inverse etc
- knowing the meaning of all symbols used at the particular level reached.

Where deaf pupils are still developing these skills, it will then be helpful if the stating of mathematical problems:

- is linguistically straightforward

The language
of mathematics

63

GUIDELINES LINK

*Promoting literacy
in deaf pupils*
RNID (2001)

- follows the order in which the operation is to be carried out
- highlights linguistic connectives where necessary such as – if, because, more than, some, together
- makes each proposition in the problem clear.

Teachers need to ensure that the classroom environment and the teaching approach have been adapted accordingly. For instance, the deaf pupil in a sign bilingual programme may depend heavily on visual access, whereas an auditory/oral or natural aural pupil will depend mainly on acoustic access. Where problems are being presented orally, visual access continues to be essential for an auditory pupil who may mishear, eg 30 as 13 or vice versa.

The classroom teacher and the teaching assistant (TA) should increase their interaction as the mathematics lessons demand more of deaf pupils in problem-solving. It is important to remember that the role of the TA is to assist the deaf pupil in accessing the mathematics curriculum. It is the class teacher who must teach and involve the deaf pupil in all class work and discussion. The deaf pupil will learn through trial and error and should be allowed to make mistakes and/or to get things right in class, receiving censure or praise on the same terms as hearing peers.

**The language
of mathematics**

Sample information for mainstream teachers

How to help the deaf pupil in your class

Remember the Chinese proverb:

Tell me and I'll forget
    Show me and I may remember – **but**
        Involve me and I will understand.

Mathematics lessons for deaf pupils in secondary education should:

- have **appropriate expectations** for each pupil

- take place in **a stimulating environment** that includes a display board for mathematics

- be **appropriately planned** to meet the needs of the pupil

- take place within the cycle of **assessment, planning, teaching and evaluation**

- have appropriate, additional **resources** available.

Planning helps to strike the right balance between the various elements of the National Numeracy Strategy and indicates the resources required to teach topics appropriately and effectively.

- Plan to revisit topics two or three times a year

- Cover three topics per half term

- Recognise that some topics may have to be missed.

Emphasise that:

- It's alright to be wrong

- It's alright to misunderstand

- It's alright to start again

- Understanding will come with time and practice.

Finally, make full use of the skills of your teaching assistant

Compiled from material contributed by LEA advisory services for deaf pupils, December 2001

Sample of problem-solving worksheet adapted for use by deaf pupils

Gardening equipment

Spades cost £9.65 each

Rakes cost £7.70 each

Flowerpots are £12.75 each

Nicola has £50.00   She buys: 3 flowerpots
                                        1 spade

How much money will Nicola have left?

Carefully:
- Read through the problem
- Underline important words

Make your calculations here:

Solve this problem here: (Process)

Put your ANSWER here:

There is some information you did not need. What was it?

Compiled from material contributed by LEA advisory services for deaf pupils, December 2001

◇ Mathematics across the curriculum

> *"The experiences of young children do not come in separate packages with 'subject labels'; as children explore the world around them, mathematical experiences present themselves alongside others. The teacher needs therefore to seek opportunities for drawing mathematical experience out of a wide range of children's activities. Very many curricular areas give rise to mathematics."*
>
> Cockcroft Report *Mathematics in the primary years Mathematics counts*
> HMSO (1982) 1997, 10th impression

Teachers should utilise every opportunity to develop a deaf pupil's mathematical perspective further and to enhance their understanding of the universal importance and practicality of mathematics when they involve them in handling and manipulating data within their subject.

Mathematical knowledge and understanding presents us with an indispensable perspective on:

- all that we experience through our senses
- the physical world
- society – both past and present.

Although teachers of mathematics teach the skills to pupils, the elements of the subject are present in all areas of the curriculum and the pupils' environment.

The National Numeracy Strategy (NNS) highlights many areas that give opportunities for developing maths across the curriculum.

Lesson tutoring in particular subjects with a focus on mathematical issues may include:

- **geography** – measuring different shapes and objects such as contour lines for hills or mountains on maps, or different sorts of measurement, eg in seismology, vulcanology, meteorology, calculating coordinates of latitude and longitude, statistics of population, rainfall etc. The difference between a compass and a set of compasses
- **craft and design technology (CDT)** – knowing the differences between estimating and accurately measuring and considering the implications of each for the particular task
- **history** – understanding time lines, issues of certainty, possibility, probability, etc, problems and dilemmas that faced countries and how they attempted to solve them
- **science** – using spatulas to carry out fine measurements etc, using scales, knowing equivalents in metric and imperial measurements, recording and organising data, interpreting the relationships between different types of

Mathematics across the curriculum

graph, understanding the significance of geological time scales, finding right and wrong ways of producing effects

- **art** – knowing names and functions of tools for measurement and drawing etc and using them appropriately
- **PE** – appreciating relative distances around the playing field, using a stop-watch for timing etc, speed and distance for running and swimming etc
- **English literature** – knowing the periods in which different authors lived, the style of language, dress, conventions, cross-cultures etc.

In this way deaf pupils are more likely to appreciate the relevance of mathematics in relation to other subjects they are studying and be able to contribute confidently while working cooperatively with others through discussion and problem-solving.

As a result of joint planning and adapted delivery, mainstream subject teachers and teachers of the deaf should highlight:

- mathematical concepts or contextualised vocabulary
- any particular mathematical challenges for access by individual deaf pupils so that appropriate planning may assist the pupil
- how well a pupil can apply mathematical skills and knowledge in subject areas so that Individual Education Plans (IEPs) reflect areas of difficulty
- an appropriate time for teaching a group, in science or mathematics lessons, about the audiogram as a greatly compressed logarithmic (decibel) scale – maybe enlisting a deaf pupil to assist
- opportunities for pupils who can use the hearing aid test box to demonstrate and explain the process, incorporating references to frequency, intensity and distortion, to groups or the whole class, eg during a science or mathematics lesson
- appropriate use of software for deaf pupils in subjects across the curriculum.

Planning in this way may also give opportunities to the teacher of the deaf to participate in departmental meetings where linguistic difficulties and mathematical aspects of a subject may be discussed. It is important to recognise that class and/or subject teachers and teachers of the deaf are learning together in terms of linguistically adapting mainstream subject lessons for access by deaf pupils in ways that preserve the conceptual content.

◇ Educational/communication approaches and the development of numeracy

This publication has deliberately avoided emphasis on communication/educational approaches, in an attempt to focus on the issues of common concern to all teachers and teaching assistants (TAS) working with deaf pupils. Short definitions of a range of approaches are included in the Glossary and readers looking for a longer consideration of different approaches are referred to on pages 12-18 of *Effective inclusion of deaf pupils into mainstream schools* (RNID 2000).

However, some communication and educational approaches bring with them particular implications for developing both literacy and numeracy. For example, sign bilingualism is developing distinctive practices to support the shift from one language, British Sign Language (BSL), to another (English) and from one mode to another (English operates in spoken and written modes while BSL has no written mode). The maternal reflective method uses written language extensively in the early years to support the acquisition of English and children using this approach are observed to pass through different characteristic stages of learning to read. Teachers using Signed English (SE) or cued speech can provide visual support to the understanding of written text in a different way to teachers and TAs using Sign Supported English (SSE).

A detailed consideration of these important issues is beyond the scope of this publication. We therefore refer readers who would like more detail on different approaches to the following sources of information:

Sign bilingualism and total communication
Peter Plant
LASER
Longwill School for the Deaf
Bell Hill
Northfield
Birmingham B31 4HA

Cued speech
Cued Speech Association UK
Corner House
Bay View
Stoke Fleming
Dartmouth TQ6 0QX

Natural auralism
Deaf Education through
Listening and Talking (DELTA)
PO Box 20
Haverhill
Suffolk CB9 7BD

Maternal reflective method
Headteacher
St John's RC School for
Hearing Impaired Children
Church Street
Boston Spa
Wetherby
West Yorkshire LS23 6DF

Educational/
communication
approaches and
the development
of numeracy

Glossary

acoustic .... of sound

applied mathematics .... related to, or put to practical use, eg mechanics and statistics

auditory-oral approaches .... teaching approaches based on the understanding that most deaf children have sufficient residual hearing to develop understanding and use of spoken language without the use of sign language or manual codes

British Sign Language (BSL) .... the language of Deaf people in the UK

cardinal number .... a number denoting quantity, eg 1, 2, 3 etc

cued speech .... a one-handed supplement to spoken language devised to clarify the phonemes of spoken language that are ambiguous or invisible in lipreading

home/school book .... a book that parents and teachers use alternately to facilitate relevant home/school conversation about a child with special educational needs or with a child with a communication difficulty

individual education plan (IEP) .... a plan setting out the targets, intended outcomes and resources for a particular pupil with special educational needs

maternal reflective method .... an approach to developing English in deaf children that uses the written word extensively to support early experiences of spoken conversation

natural auralism .... an auditory-oral approach to fostering the development of spoken language through meaningful interaction and conversation using residual hearing rather than through direct teaching

ordinal number................................a number defining position in order, eg first, second etc

personal FM system ....a radio system that extends the range over which a speaker's voice is transmitted to the receiver worn by the pupil

phenomena ....plural of phenomenon

phenomenon................................fact or event

pure mathematics ....mathematics studied for its theoretical aspects rather than its practical aspects, eg algebra (arithmetic), geometry and logic

soundfield system ....an FM system that amplifies a speaker's voice in a room

total communication................................a teaching approach which may use British Sign Language (BSL), Sign Supported English (SSE), Signed English (SE) and/or fingerspelling as well as spoken and written English.

Bibliography

Arnold P
Mathematics and Deafness in Deafness and Development 1 (2)
(1990-91)

Barham J
Helping your deaf child with mathematics
NDCS (1990)

Bunch Gary Owen
The curriculum and the hearing-impaired student
Theoretical and practical considerations
College Hill – Little Brown and Co (1987)

Cockcroft W H
Mathematics Counts – Cockcroft Report
HMSO (1982) 1997, 10th impression

Gregory S, Knight P et al
Issues in deaf education
David Fulton (1998)

Kluwin T N, Moores D F, Gaustad M G
Toward effective public school programmes for deaf students
Teachers' College Press NY (1992)

Leutke-Stahlman B
Language across the Curriculum
When students are deaf or hard of hearing
Butte Publications Inc Oregon (1999)

Leutke-Stahlman B and Luckner J
Effectively educating students with hearing impairments
Longman NY 1991

Mousley K, Kelly R R
Problem-solving strategies for teaching mathematics to deaf students
American Annals of the Deaf 143 (4) (1998)

National Numeracy Strategy
DfEE (1999)

National Strategy – Key Stage 3
DfEE (2001)

Nunes T
Developing children's minds through literacy and numeracy
University of London (1998)

Nunes T and Moreno C
The signed algorithm and its bugs
Educational studies in mathematics 35 (1998)

Nunes T and Moreno C
Is hearing impairment a cause of difficulty in learning mathematics?
EQUALS 3 (1) (1997)

Pagliaro C
Mathematics reform in the education of deaf and hard of hearing students
American Annals of the Deaf Vol. 143 (1998)

Powers S, Gregory S et al
A review of good practice in deaf education
RNID (1999)

Ross M
Hearing impaired children in the mainstream
York Press (1990)

Stewart D A and Kluwin T N
Teaching deaf and hard of hearing students
Content, strategies and curriculum
Allyn & Bacon (2001)

Acknowledgements

RNID is grateful to the following government bodies, organisations, LEAs, schools and individuals for their contribution to the development of these Education Guidelines materials.

The National Numeracy Strategy
London House
59-65 London Street
Reading
RG1 4EW

Qualifications and Curriculum Authority (QCA)
29 Borland Street
London
EC1Y 8SL
www.qca.org.uk

British Association of Teachers of the Deaf (BATOD)
21 The Haystacks
High Wycombe
Buckinghamshire
HP13 6PY
www.batod.org.uk

British Deaf Association
1-3 Worship Street
London
EC2A 2AB

Cued Speech Association UK
Corner House
Bay View
Stoke Fleming
Dartmouth
TQ6 0QX

Deaf Education through Listening and Talking Association (DELTA)
DELTA
PO Box 20
Haverhill
Suffolk
CB9 7BD

Birmingham Visiting Teacher Service
Vauxhall Gardens
Barrack Street
Birmingham
B7 4HA

Derby – Royal School for the Deaf
Ashbourne Road
Derby
DE22 3BH

Devon Hearing Support Centre
Glasshouse Lane
Countess Wear
Exeter
EX2 7BS

Fife – Service for Children and Young People with Sensory Impairment
Auchterderran Centre
Cardende
Fife KY5 0NE

Frank Barnes Primary School for Deaf Children
Harley Road
Swiss Cottage
London
NW3 3BN

Hamilton Lodge School for Deaf Children
Walpole Road
Brighton
BN2 7BJ

Herefordshire – Physical and Sensory Support Service
Education Department
PO Box 185
Blackfriars Street
Hereford
HR4 9ZR

Humberside Hearing Impaired Service
Lowfield Lane
Melton
Kingston-upon-Hull
HU14 3HT

Kent – Royal School for Deaf Children Margate
Victoria Road
Margate
Kent
CT9 1NB

Longwill School for the Deaf
Bell Hill
Northfield
Birmingham
B31 1LD

Oxfordshire Sensory Support Service
The Wheatley Centre
Littleworth Road
Wheatley
Oxon
OX33 1PH

Solihull Support Team for Hearing Impaired Children
Reynalds Cross
Kineton Green Road
Solihull
B92 7ER

St John's Catholic School for the Deaf
Boston Spa
Wetherby
West Yorkshire
LS23 6DF

Surrey Service for Hearing Impaired Children
The Lodge, Glyn House
Church Street
Ewell
Surrey
KT17 2AP

Wolverhampton Service for Hearing Impaired Children
The Jennie Lee Centre
Lichfield Road
Wednesfield
Wolverhampton
WV11 3HT

Worcestershire Service for Children with Sensory Impairments
17 Castle Street
Worcester
WR1 3AD

Wandsworth Service for Hearing Impaired Children
Oak Lodge School
101 Nightingale Lane
London
SW12 8NA

Sue Bainbridge
National Numeracy Strategy

Claire Holland and colleagues
DfES

Joy Jarvis
University of Hertfordshire

Paul Simpson
BATOD

Additional thanks are due to the following schools and services where photographs were taken.

Frank Barnes Primary School for Deaf Children
Harley Road
Swiss Cottage
London
NW3 3BN

Hamilton Lodge School for Deaf Children
Walpole Road
Brighton
BN2 2ET

Ovingdean Hall School
Greenways
Brighton
BN2 7BJ

Oxfordshire – Sensory Support Service
The Wheatley Centre
Littleworth Road
Wheatley
Oxon
OX33 1PH